An Introduction to
3 DIMENSIONAL LEADERSHIP

A Framework for Leadership Development

Nigel Linacre & Jefferson Cann

First published by Extraordinary Leadership, 2011
www.xleadership.com

Extraordinary Leadership, 51 St Mary Street, Chippenham, Wilts SN15 3JW, UK. info@xleadership.com

Text Copyright: Nigel Linacre and Jefferson Cann 2011

All rights reserved. Except for brief quotations in critical articles or reviews, no part of this book may be reproduced in any manner without prior written permission from the publishers.

The rights of Nigel Linacre and Jefferson Cann as authors have been asserted in accordance with the Copyright, Designs and Patents Act 1988.

Design by Julia East 2011

Printed and bound by CPI Group (UK) Ltd, Croydon, CR0 4YY

The Authors

Nigel Linacre and Jefferson Cann enable leadership development for individuals, teams and organizations via the firm they founded, Extraordinary Leadership[1] which works in Europe and America, Asia and Africa.

Both experienced leadership coaches, they began their work together in Kenya by taking leaders on Extraordinary Leadership Journeys based in and around rural schools. The learnings they gathered there now form the basis of their unique approach to leadership development in offices and meeting rooms across the world.

They are two of the four founding trustees of WellBoring[2]; a membership-based charity which provides sustainable water solutions to African schools and communities.

Nigel Linacre's business and philosophical titles include *The Successful Executive*, *Recipes for Happiness*, and *Why You Are Here – Briefly*. His leadership reflections appear in the International Leadership Association's 2012 volume, Leading in Complex Worlds.

Acknowledgments

We are privileged to work with great clients in great depth. The opportunity of working with them continually enriches us and our work.

We would like to acknowledge the contribution of our colleagues, Anne Stenbom, Chris Monk, Eithne Wright and Helen Battersby, as well as Kate Cann and Susie Linacre, on our work.

---

[1] See www.xleadership.com
[2] See www.WellBoring.org

Contents

The Authors 3
Preface 6
Introduction 7

A FRAMEWORK FOR LEADERSHIP 8
Introducing 3-Dimensional Leadership....................................9
Introducing 9 Forms of Leadership 11
The 3 Dimensions...13
Being a Leader..14
Leadership through Space 17
Leadership in Time 19

THE 9 FORMS OF LEADERSHIP 21
Authentic Leadership 24
Journeying Leadership 27
Inspired Leadership..29
Adult Leadership..33
Coaching Leadership 36
Inspirational Leadership...39
Grounded Leadership 42
Challenging Leadership 44
Visionary Leadership 46
A Preliminary 3-Dimensional Profile.....................................49

3-DIMENSIONAL LEADERSHIP DEVELOPMENT 52
Authentic Leadership Development......................................59
Journeying Leadership Development 61
Inspired Leadership Development 63
Adult Leadership Development...65

Coaching Leadership Development 67
Inspirational Leadership Development 69
Grounded Leadership Development 71
Challenging Leadership Development 73
Visionary Leadership Development 75

APPENDICES 78
Lines of Leadership 79
Bibliography 86
Leadership and Time Management 87
Liberating Leadership 88
3-D Leadership and Emotional Intelligence 89
3-Dimensional Leadership and the Integral Model 90
Towards a Common Framework for Leadership 91
The New Leaders and 3-D Leadership 92
Warren Bennis and 3-D Leadership 93
Leadership and Values 94
A Word on Leadership Development 95

Preface

This is an Introduction to 3-Dimensional Leadership.

3-Dimensional Leadership has developed from our extensive work and experience in leadership development. We feel that through this lens, we provide a new and uniquely comprehensive approach to developing the integrated, connected, whole-being leadership so sorely needed by the world to cope with the challenges over the coming decades. We offer these perspectives in the full understanding that they are subject to validation and refinement and look forward to working on this in the future.

That having been said, the dimensions of Time and Space are real for us all, and the dimension of action is the arena of the leader. The ideas and the Forms of Leadership have been tried and tested in workshops and with individual leaders. They have the merit that they can be readily understood, making the field of leadership itself more accessible; and that is our purpose.

While we accept that models must be robust, we try to be mindful that they are only descriptions, and their value comes in their use. With that in mind, we look forward to receiving feedback from leaders and those interested in leadership.

Introduction

Only you can develop yourself as a leader. 3D Leadership provides a context for you to explore your unique leadership abilities.

Leadership remains somewhat stuck in the feudal era: I'll follow you. We tend to equate leadership with whoever appears to be in charge. But we are all leaders now: in our work, homes, and communities. And the information age requires local decision-making, and what has been called "distributed leadership[3]".

And organizations want a different kind of leadership. They want communities of leaders who can all take initiatives and make a difference, without waiting to be asked. Local leaders provide local leadership! And leadership emerges as and when needed in each situation.

3-Dimensional Leadership offers a map of leadership. You'll discover 9 Forms of Leadership, and be better placed to decide how you want to develop yourself as a leader. You can get to it fast, skipping footnotes[4] and leaving appendices until another day. We have tended to simplify and generalize. You can add your own caveats.

For each of the forms, we include some suggestions for developing your leadership, using them is your choice. No-one else can make you lead.

Welcome to the next stage in your leadership journey.

---

[3] See the Sloan School of Management.
[4] Our Leadership workshops are mainly experiential. Theory merely provides context, something to hang your thoughts on. 3-Dimensional Leadership Development is just another context – it is what you do with it that will make the difference.

A FRAMEWORK FOR LEADERSHIP

Introducing 3Dimensional Leadership

Leadership lacks a common framework. A range of definitions, alleged styles, and limited thinking make it hard to become a leader. There's too much smoke.

We want to make becoming a leader more straightforward. In three dimensional leadership, leaders work in time and space. We highlight three steps in each dimension, starting with:

- **Time:** Leaders usher in the future[5]. They connect with what's going on Now, plus a Future, and the Path from Now into the Future. So we focus on three moments: Now, Path and the Future.

- **Space:** Leaders affect a world beyond themselves. First they lead them-Selves, then they work through their Team to affect that world; Self, Team[6] and World are three spatial milestones.

- **Action:** Leaders start by being Aware, because nothing happens without awareness, then they Connect and then they Transform. Without Awareness, leaders can't Connect, and without Connection they can't Transform: which gives us "ACT" for short.

Leaders always work within these 3 dimensions. For example, a leader may work on their own Self-Awareness in the present moment, Connect with a Team's Path, and then Transform a Future vision for the World they affect.

If you need to see how this fits together now, skip ahead to page 22.

---

[5] We capitalize words that have a special meaning in 3D Leadership.
[6] We use "Team" and "Others" meaning all those through whom a leader works interchangeably.

In each case the leader operates intentionally. Visually this looks like:

	Now	The Way	Future
The World			Transform Future Vision of the World they affect
The Team		Connecting with the Team's Path	
The Self	Working on Self-Awareness In the present moment		

Chart 1: A leader working in several leadership spaces.

We show time running horizontally and space vertically. Imagine Awareness on a top sheet, Connection behind it, and Transformation behind that. In the examples just given, the leader starts in the lower left, moves onto the middle space and then to the top right.

Leaders work with all these spaces, each of which calls for a different "Form of Leadership"[7].

---

[7] If you viewed this 3-Dimensionally, you would see a total of 27 spaces (3 x 3 x 3).

Introducing 9 Forms of Leadership

You will see 9 Forms of Leadership on the back cover.

We say each Form[8] of Leadership is appropriate to a time and space. In each Form we work with Awareness, Connection and Transformation.

However you lead, you can utilize all 9 Forms of Leadership. Working with them you remain free to choose how you lead in each space. Anyone can develop their capabilities in each Form.

You will have heard of some of them. We may all want to be Authentic Leaders, Inspiring Leaders and Visionary Leaders, if only we knew what they were or how they became so. As you will see, Authentic Leaders are able to be themselves in the present moment, Inspiring Leaders are able to see the Future Potential in others, and Visionary Leaders can see a version of the uncreated future.

You may already suppose Coaching, Challenging and being Inspired are aspects of leadership. We say that Coaching Leaders enable their team to move along a path. Challenging Leaders anticipate and respond to upcoming problems, challenging the complacency of the status quo. And Inspired Leaders are inspired by their own future potential, whatever their current shortcomings.

We include three more Forms of Leadership that may be less familiar but are in our view no less important. Grounded Leaders connect with the present moment. They see what is happening in the here and now. Adult Leaders work with others, with their team, on the basis of professional, "Adult-to-Adult" respect. Journeying Leaders know that they are on a Journey of their own, continually seeking to develop themselves and their ability to relate to others and their world.

---

[8] We call them "Forms" to convey that leadership is one whole thing, while the different forms depend on time and space. Individually they may be called "Types of Leadership", but we are uncomfortable with "Styles" of leadership, which flies in the face of authenticity: real leadership is not a style.

Do you have an immediate sense of where you are currently strong? Try selecting intuitively three Forms of Leadership you believe are your relative strengths, and three you believe are your relative weaknesses[9].

Is there a pattern to your strengths? Are most of them in the present? Are they mainly at the level of the Team? You may see that you can begin to navigate leadership right away. For leaders, self-reflection is a valuable practice in and of itself.

Thinking of your immediate peers, where is each of them strongest? For each of them can you identify a blind spot, an aspect of leadership they may not have even noticed? Some of their leadership strengths and weaknesses may be immediately obvious to you.

Now you can get practical. If you could develop just one Form of Leadership, what would that be? And why that is important to you?

You have a provisional view of yourself and perhaps others. But how do others see you? You will find more at *www.xleadership/3D*.

---

[9] This isn't a direct comparison with others – you may be stronger or weaker than someone else all round. This is just about your relative strengths.

The 3 Dimensions

If you want to explore the three dimensions themselves, stay with the narrative for the next dozen pages and explore:

- Being a Leader
- Leadership through Space
- Leadership in Time

If you want to go straight to a more detailed look at the 9 Forms of Leadership next, simply skip to the following section.

Being a Leader

How a leader is being determines how a leader behaves. For example, how you feel affects the way you behave. Your inner voice makes a huge difference to your performance: How you are - your "being" - is the foundation of how you behave, which is the cause of results.

When we contemplate being, it all starts with Awareness. For leaders we highlight Awareness of Self, Team and World. A leader who's unaware of something won't be able to change it.

What are you aware of in yourself right now? You may notice your breathing (physical), the thoughts that rush across the screen of your mind (mental), and how you are feeling (emotional). You may even be aware of why you are reading this book - your purpose (spiritual)[10].

Awareness

Let's start with Awareness: If you've completed an Emotional Intelligence ("EI") profile you may remember hearing of Self-Awareness[11] and Awareness of Others. We also apply Awareness to the World you affect. So leaders may be Aware of Self, Team and World. As well as the present moment, we say leaders are Aware of the potential future, which they can also Connect with and Transform (right and middle columns).

Awareness informs leadership in all 9 spaces. It provides the platform for a leader to connect with themselves, their people and the world they inhabit. Without awareness, there can be no Connection. You may notice when you've really connected

---

[10] You can think of physical, mental, emotional and spiritual as four planes of being.

[11] Awareness is a well-established concept in Emotional Intelligence in the forms of Self-Awareness and Awareness of others. It describes and measures your tendency to be in touch with your body, your feelings and your intuitions, while Awareness of Others measures your tendency to be in touch with the feeling states of others.

with a member of your team: you've got it, they've got it, and communication is perfect.

Connection

Now let's turn to Connection: like Awareness, Connection starts with the Self, if you don't connect with who you are others won't either. The need to connect applies to all the other Forms of Leadership. So it includes Connection with the World you affect, plus the Future and Path. Research has shown that we are "hardwired" for connection[12].

Let's take a practical example. You may Connect with the absence of something in the present world and start to deeply Connect with it as a possibility in the Future, in other words, develop a Vision. So you started in the top left of the chart and moved to the top right. A leader who doesn't Connect is lost, and, literally, ends up speaking to themselves.

Transformation

Leaders Transform! Anything else falls short of a complete leadership process. Important as it is, optimizing what already exists is management, although all management can contain within it aspects of leadership. We use the word "Transformation" in two senses: everything a leader does to enable Transformation, and the resulting Transformation itself. Transformation has occurred when:

– There is a new space, an expansion in one's perception that provides a new relationship to self and the world

– There are new perspectives and understandings

– A sense of increased harmony and connections (inner and outer)

– Something new, beyond the old conception of the self and

---

[12] See www.ted.com/speakers/brene_brown.html

its original intentions, emerges

- Others' responses witness that there has been a profound change

Many of us arrive in what we might think of as a leadership position, Managing Director, for example, and then work hard to survive at this new level. But surviving isn't leading.

Consider how you can practice Awareness, Connection and Transformation through the Four Levels of Being[13]:

- Physical: The ability to manage your physical state, to be able move from a state of potential stress or fear to a state of dynamic relaxation, or "flow", for optimal performance and the fulfilment of potential.

- Mental: To remain clear-sighted and rational without losing the ability to connect at the human level - to maintain a high level of emotional intelligence focussed on the benefit of the greater good.

- Emotional: To acknowledge your emotional reactions, understand their purpose and to integrate them into balanced, emotionally intelligent, Adult-to-Adult interactions with those involved in all circumstances, rooted in a clear perception of the present without regret for the past or fear for the future.

- Spiritual: To know the purpose of your actions, and how this purpose fulfils your sense of meaning and that of those your actions effect up to the broadest level of your "world".

---

[13] We have seen them described elsewhere as the four dimensions of being. As we are focusing on the dimensions of leadership, we have adopted levels to minimise confusion.

Leadership through Space

Let's take a trip through space. Leadership starts with leadership of the self. If you can't lead yourself, you can't lead others. This is the foundation of leadership[14].

Starting with Self-leadership

Why is this? First, leaders who are unable to lead themselves cannot walk the talk, and so are unable to lead by example. They are trying to do leadership but haven't become a leader. They say what they want you to do but don't do it themselves – so you do it, but you do it half-heartedly – undermining team performance. It may not be said to their face, but they will be unconvincing.

Second, if you are unable to lead yourself you won't know how to lead others, you won't have the base in place, as you can't give to others what you don't have. Not seeing your potential, you're unlikely to see theirs, and so on.

A Basis for Leading Teams

Leadership of self is not all. Leaders accomplish though others. Leaders do make time to reflect on their own, and go out into the world they affect to see what is happening, what may be about to happen and what could happen, but they spend most of their time with their teams. This is how they make the most of their difference. They are Aware of, Connect with and Transform team performance. They work with them as they are ("Adult"), work with them on the obstacles ("Coaching") and sensing their potential ("Inspirational").

If you want to find a good leader, find a good team; if you want to find a great leader, find a great team.

---

[14] Consequently we say Leadership Development must begin with leadership of the self, without which further development is not possible.

And Affecting the World

Leaders also look outwards at the world that they affect. For the point of the leader and the team is to affect a part of the world beyond the team, to contribute in some way, to make a difference. Without that, the team is pointless.

They're Aware of the World as it is, deeply Connect with it and look to Transform it, all of which is Grounded Leadership. The same applies to the rapids that must be navigated, (Challenging Leadership). As important as noticing what does exist, they notice what does not exist, and could, which provides the Awareness within Visionary Leadership.

There's a symbiosis between leader, team and world. The leader serves themselves and the team: who would want to follow a leader who didn't care for the Team[15]? We propose Teams don't need such leaders.

Similarly, leaders and their Teams are there to serve the World they affect. Does the World need leaders who don't care for it[16]?

---

[15] In an age of coercion, we had no option but to follow our leaders. In this age of discovery, we choose to follow or to leave our leaders.

[16] UK company directors now have a legal responsibility to a company's stakeholders only one group of which is the shareholders. Finding win-win-win solutions, for the leader, team and wider world, is the leader's quest.

Leadership in Time

Leaders usher in the Future. We say that leaders work with Now, the Path and the Future. Now is vital, but what about the Path and the Future, and why not the Past?

Starting with the Now

Let's start now. Temporally, everything starts Now, and we recognize that "Being here now" is really important. We may often be somewhere in our imagination, in our fears, in our idle speculations. If a leader doesn't get what's happening now – by which we mean an Awareness of the overall picture for Self, Team and World; the trends, the key numbers – they won't be able to influence well or make good decisions. In short, they won't get it. If you don't know where you are, you don't know where you are going.

A Leap into the Future

Leaders create the Future. The rest of us wait until it turns up. They are creating the Future for them Selves, Team and World. While this uncreated Future doesn't yet exist in the external world, it already exists in the internal world, in the imagination of the leader. They dare to dream, as leaders often do.

Notice that everything changes. A little more dramatically, everything is born and dies. The way Leader, Team and World are now is just a temporary phenomenon. The future awaits your intentions.

Their vision of their future self they may keep to themselves. Their vision for their team they will seek to instil in the Team. When the time is propitious, they will share their vision of the World with the Team, sufficient for them to get it, even though they will translate it into their own terms.

Future Leadership includes Inspired Leadership, Inspirational Leadership and Visionary Leadership (bottom, middle and top). An Inspired Leader sees their own potential, an Inspirational

Leader sees your potential and enables you to Connect with it too, while a Visionary Leader lets you to see the difference you can make to the World; and that is what it's all about.

Navigating the Path

Leaders go into the Future before considering the Path. If you don't know where you are going, all paths may look the same. Sensing the present and unswervingly focusing on the future, a Leader is ready to address the Path, even though it may be seen but dimly. In truth, it is more like a series of paths, each of them with their own attendant risks and possibilities. Sensing the path provides the possibility of anticipating opportunity and danger. Leaders know there is a Path, in fact a multitude of them, ready to be navigated, for Leaders themselves, the Team and the World they affect. All have their own urgency and importance[17]. The Path is a means to an end.

And the past? We carry it in our conditioned responses[18]. We continually recreate it: we think, feel and do the same stuff and often spend time looking back saying we're "analyzing" events when all we are doing is trying to re-arrange our view of them to make ourselves feel more comfortable or escape the blame of others or ourselves.

Leaders help us escape from the past. Leaders know it's gone and move forward on the basis of the lessons learned. They drop, and help us drop, the "burden" of the past so that we can move to the fulfillment of our vision, our preferred future, more easily and efficiently.

---

[17] See the Appendix on Leadership and Time Management.
[18] Remember Pavlov's dogs? Pavlov rang a bell and fed the dogs, and did this again and again, until as soon as he rang the bell they started to salivate even in the absence of food.

THE 9 FORMS OF LEADERSHIP

The 9 Forms of Leadership

Looking at time and space, we find that each of the 9 spaces has a specific form of leadership that we can explore:

	Now	Path	Future
World	Grounded Leadership	Challenging Leadership	Visionary Leadership
Team	Adult Leadership	Coaching Leadership	Inspiring Leadership
Self	Authentic Leadership	Journeying Leadership	Inspired Leadership

Self Leadership

For us, all leadership begins with leadership of the self. So we start with three forms of self-leadership:

- Authentic Leadership
- Journeying Leadership
- Inspired Leadership

Authentic Leadership

Authentic Leaders walk their talk. Because their leadership is an expression of who they are, leadership comes naturally to them.

So leadership is not something they do: it is who they are. They don't decide to "do some leadership". They aren't being inauthentic, for example trying to present an image to the world that is at odds with who they really are. Authentic leaders are getting on with the business of being themselves.

These leaders direct themselves. They are self-aware, self-connected and self-transformational. They can rely on others but they are content to rely on themselves. Because they are authentic, they lead by example. Authentic Leadership is the cornerstone of all leadership. That's why it's the base of the 9 Forms of Leadership: it's about leading yourself (bottom row) in the present moment (left hand column).

Authentic leaders have got something: a knowledge of themselves and their beliefs. More than that, they have an acceptance of themselves; a knowing of what they stand for. Authentic Leadership is also exemplary leadership.

And because they are OK with themselves they are likely to be OK with others. That's why Authentic Leadership provides a foundation for Adult Leadership, and it informs Grounded Leadership. Looking horizontally, Authentic Leadership informs Journeying and Inspired Leadership. Knowing yourself is a key to knowing your potential or ideal self, and making that transition[19].

Within Authentic Leadership, let's start with self-awareness: what are you aware of about yourself right now? How's your breathing, what's happening on the screenplay of your mind, what emotions are you experiencing, and how is your sense of purpose? Thinking about Connection: what do you stand for, what do you believe in, what values have you been demonstrating in the way you have been leading yourself last week? And what values will you demonstrate today?

---

[19] 'Know Thyself' is famously inscribed over the threshold to the Oracle of Delphi in Ancient Greece (c. 500BC).

Many of us often experience blockages at all four aspects of life: physiologically, mentally, emotionally, spiritually[20]. During a meeting, we may be unaware of how we are feeling, merely sensing a little comfort or discomfort. We may be having a fantasy of our own about whether people like us. Or we may be gripped by a negative fantasy that causes us to feel fear or anxiety. In none of those cases are we here now. We are not able to be authentic to the moment.

How do you develop your Authentic Leadership? Make time to get to know yourself. If you experience a reluctance to get to know yourself, the case for doing so is stronger. Get a clearer sense of your strengths and weaknesses and be OK with them. Explore your values and beliefs. Reflect on who you are and what you are about. Try to differentiate between the push motivations that others have offered you – for example, well-intentioned relatives and friends – and your own deeper motivations: get to know them. This is not the work of a day: it is the work of a lifetime.

What are inauthentic leaders like? They don't walk their talk, perhaps because their talk is not really theirs: it is what they think they should say. They don't know what their values are. They are trying to look like leaders without having done the necessary internal work on themselves. They may imagine that their title means they have magically become a leader.

You can't work on something when you are in denial! As soon as you are Aware of an aspect of your character, as soon as you accept it without judgment, you can start to change. Until that point, nothing is possible.

It is actually the unacknowledged aspects of self that get in the way. By disowning aspects of ourselves, by trying to lock our fears up in a box, we find ourselves distracted. We remain uncomfortable with ourselves. And this discomfort is of course sensed by others, limiting our ability to lead. This lack of self-acceptance makes transformation impossible.

---

[20] We use "spiritual" to mean having to do with meaning and purpose, whatever that is for you. Those who assert that life is meaningless may be asked: what is the point of leadership?

Authentic Leaders have worked through this stuff. They are aware of who they are and are OK about themselves because they have accepted who they are[21]. Their Connection with themselves communicates itself towards others, and, whether they are loud or quiet, introvert or extrovert, this connection is the basis of charisma. They may regard their talents as gifts that they are of course happy to share.

Their acceptance of self opens the door to Transformation.

---

[21] One can develop personal awareness and not be OK with who you are, i.e. have low self-regard, but that's not a good place to be; it's also completely unnecessary.

Journeying Leadership

Journeying Leaders reinvent themselves. They are actively engaged in self-development. By developing themselves over many years, they move a long way ahead.

Actually, everyone gets reinvented. Are you the same person you were when you were ten or twenty years old? How have you changed? Most of us think and feel differently. Though some aspects of character tend to remain, we are all different.

Journeying Leaders go further. They know their future self will be different too. The self they currently inhabit is just themselves at a moment in time. Journeying Leaders know that they are on, well, a Journey. While they have come some distance, they know they aren't there yet. Indeed, they never get there, because there is no destination, just a continuing journey[22]. Because leaders act upon the world, it is first and foremost an inner journey into greater Awareness, Connection and Transformation.

They notice themselves and sense they are changing: in fact they realize that not changing simply is not possible. They are aware of at least some of their own weaknesses and they are working on them.

Since they are always learning, they are unlikely to need to defend their point of view, though they may choose to do so: it is, after all, just a point of view. This flexibility enables them to be open to others' views. While they are really interested in what's true, they are more interested in the truth that may be discovered in the next conversation. As they know their own views are developing, hanging on to them may impede progress.

Journeying Leaders develop themselves in different ways. You may develop your areas of brilliance or shore up weaknesses, work on beliefs and values or operational skills, develop your general knowledge or focus on one particular area. They are all valid choices. Working on your own leadership development is a Journeying Leadership activity.

---

[22] Etymologically, Journey means day. With the benefit of this insight, life is a succession of journeys.

What would you most like to change about the way you lead? What new habits would make the biggest difference to your performance? What would you most like to give to others that you don't? What new skills would you most like to develop? How do others want you to change?

In all cases, Journeying Leaders chart their own course on their own journey. They are committed to self-development to be more effective leaders and to discover more of themselves.

You might be a little thrown by the idea that every aspect of your self may change. However, something rather magical often happens to people who realize that everything tangible about themselves may change: they form a deeper connection with something deeper, which we call the "continuing self", the part of you that was you when you were a child and is still you now, whatever that may be.

Your future self awaits you.

Inspired Leadership

Inspired Leaders inspire themselves. They may not be inspired by the person they currently are, but they are inspired by the potential they have yet to realize. They sense a future self that is – or could be – absolutely amazing; unlimited and unknown.

They don't believe they are perfect. Far from it, they know they can be better, and that better leader already exists in their mind. That imaginary self feels real, and they are moving towards its realization. Learning and development professionals talk about realizing human potential. That is what Inspired Leaders do, starting with themselves.

Having sensed this potential in themselves, they are likely to sense the potential in others. Consequently, Inspired Leadership provides the foundation for Inspirational Leadership. Before you inspire others you have to be inspired yourself, since you can't give what you don't have. Or as some would put it, you can't give to others what you don't give to yourself.

Like the two other forms of future leadership – Inspirational and Visionary Leadership – its focus is the as yet unrealized future potential[23] or possibilities. It requires an act of the imagination even to go there.

Where have you already been brilliant and where would you like to become brilliant? What does your future self look like to you and what would you love yourself to become? If you had one super-talent that you would love to give to the world, what would it be? Dare to dream as leaders often do!

Another way to approach this is to consider: what does your world need, and how can you help to get it some of that? What could your leadership role be?

Inspired[24] Leadership is the future form of Self Leadership.

---

[23] In Learning & Development, as well as the broader corporate world, we talk about realising or unlocking potential.

[24] To inspire literally means to breathe in (just as to expire means to breath out): as a basis for being more inspired, you may want to pay more attention to your breathing and breathe more deeply, which of course helps to produce a calmness.

It is informed by Authentic Leadership and provides the direction and goal for Journeying Leadership and in turn inspires them. There's a symbiotic development.

Inspired Leaders have no idea what they can't accomplish. Even if they can't complete it today, it may be accomplished tomorrow. Their sense of their potential is that it is unlimited. Notice what you think you would never be able to accomplish, and that's the problem.

Most of us shy away from seeing greatness in ourselves, even in our potential, for several reasons. Greatness is outside our comfort zone. We wonder who are we to imagine greatness[25], and we rule ourselves out of the picture. We may fear that the pack will criticize us for aiming to – in some sense – rise above them. We may fear failure and even judge ourselves for not having already got there: if we can be great, why aren't we great yet?

If there is some distance to go to discover our greatness – as the Journeying Leader recognizes – then there is a measure of freedom. And one of the ways to discover that freedom is to think in terms of meaning and purpose.

Consider your mission. We take the view that you can have more than one mission – a professional mission, a social mission, and so on – and you can have different missions in different periods of your life. Our assumption is that you get to choose your mission – it's not predestined for you – but even if it were you would have to discover it! And of course you can vary and refine your mission over a period of time. You can even start all over again. One archetypal mission statement reads, "To live, to love, to leave a legacy[26]". What's yours, or what would yours be? And if you don't know your purpose, gently and with respect, who does know it?

How do Inspired Leaders get beyond their current selves?

---

[25] As Marianne Williamson wrote, "We ask ourselves, 'Who am I to be brilliant, gorgeous, talented, fabulous?' Who are you not to be? Your timidity does not serve the world."

[26] We first came across this formulation in Stephen Covey's "7 Habits of Highly Effective People".

Let's imagine you are here for a reason: what is it? What difference would you love to make? Life provides a space for purpose; meaning is vital to leadership – imagine a purposeless leader.

Inspired Leaders sense a field of possibilities. They can give themselves to a higher purpose, because the ego is less present. Inspired Leadership includes awareness of the uncreated self. Inspired Leaders have realized that greatness is for all. They are well-set for Inspirational Leadership. Seeing greatness in their potential-selves, they may more easily see it in others.

Leading Others

Having taken a tour through leadership of the self we are better placed to review the way we lead others. We introduce three forms of leading others:

– Adult Leadership
– Coaching Leadership
– Inspirational Leadership

All three of them are vital to being a 3-Dimensional Leader.

Adult Leadership

Adult[27] Leaders get great performance from others. In the modern economy where information and decision-making are dispersed, this means that you are able to treat your team like adults who are capable of making their own decisions for their areas. You want them to be brilliant.

We may want to be treated like an Adult, and we may want to treat others as though they are adults. But strangely we often don't. We try to control others as though they are children. Sometimes *we* surrender control to others as though we are children, disempowering ourselves and putting pressure on our leader who may now have too much on their plate.

Leaders work with others. If you can't work well with others, you can't lead well. In today's economy, most people don't have to follow a particular leader[28]. They can leave, and they often do. As has been remarked elsewhere, "People join companies, they leave managers".

So the 'Command and Control' approach must be used sparingly: the best people – those who really want to give the most – walk soonest when subjected to this potentially dictatorial approach; which doesn't mean that the vision won't be clear and parameters set.

Adult Leadership describes how leaders can work with others in the present moment: in an Adult-to-Adult way. While leaders still take responsibility for the decisions made, relations are conducted on the basis of mutual respect. Who knows where the next great idea will come from? Adult Leaders claim no monopoly on wisdom – which would only slow the whole process down – they expect team members to contribute powerfully. Another term for Adult-to-Adult is "professional".

---

[27] The Adult-to-Adult reference and the adult in Adult Leadership is borrowed from Transactional Analysis, a brilliant model of functional and dysfunctional human relationships: see "Games that People Play", by Eric Berne.

[28] "People join organisations and leave managers" according to Buckingham et al "First Break All The Rules".

By contrast, Parent-to-Child is like: "I know, you don't, do it my way." In the short-term it is can be expedient. For example, when there is a crisis in which there simply isn't sufficient time to explain: like a building on fire. Even then, an Adult Leader will do this as a matter of conscious choice rather than an unconscious reaction.

How do you usually behave towards your reports? The basis of the knowledge economy is that we each see parts of the picture. We have to share equally in order to see the full picture. A leader who others feel intimidated by will never see the whole picture. For example, think about your own response to these questions:

- What does being in a controlling parent mode feel like to you?
- What tends to push you in that direction?
- What are the consequences when you take charge? How do you imagine others feel?
- How do you feel when others tell you how to do your job?
- What is it like when you go into controlled child?
- What tends to cause you to go there?
- How could you keep yourself in adult mode?

Adult leaders are secure enough in their relations with others that they can be vulnerable. They can admit they don't know. They can ask you what you think and be influenced by you.

Good Authentic Leaders who are secure in themselves are of course likely to be good Adult Leaders too. Just as in Emotional Intelligence, those with high self-awareness are likely to be aware of others. They will be more open to others, but if you are insecure in yourself you are likely to close things off.

As the name suggests, Adult Leaders connect with others in a mutually respectful, Adult-to-Adult way.

Adult leaders give others the best they can and get the best from them. Adult Leaders value others as much as they value themselves. They won't ask others to do what they wouldn't do themselves.

As in Transactional Analysis, there is no need to adopt either parental or childlike ways of behaving[29]. The Adult Leader is aware of, connects with and enables other to transform. Connection includes having good relations with others. Transformation means getting the best from them. Now the Adult Leader can engage from a place of truth.

If you cannot access and maintain the Adult space within yourself, you cannot truly lead others - you will only react and coerce, however subtly you may do so.

---

[29] When we seek to control other grown-ups, we could be said to be acting in a parental controlling way, which is only occasionally appropriate, e.g. when we must immediately evacuate a building because there is a fire. When others give control to a leader, they can be said to be behaving in a controlled child way, and the leader will no longer get their best efforts, just subservience.

Coaching Leadership

Leaders continually prompt their team members to develop. Coaching is one of the most powerful ways of doing that, and a leader's own actions are of course a key means of coaching others by example.

Coaching Leadership sits in the middle of the 9 Forms of Leadership. It connects[30] where team members are now with their potential. It enables them to navigate the forthcoming challenges in their journey from the present to the desired future.

We like to say that if you want to find a great leader, find a great team. But teams don't always start as great teams, and development takes time. Coaching Leaders find time for their team.

Good coaching enables people to become aware of the choices they can make. It doesn't take responsibility away from people. It turns out that we are often hemmed in by our limited awareness of our situation. We sometimes imagine we are stuck. Coaching triggers Awareness of options, Connection with potential, and personal and situational Transformation.

Coaches do this mainly by asking questions. While the actual questions depend upon individual circumstances, they often include questions like: "What do you want to be different? What will that look like? What difference will that make? Why is that important to you? What has to happen for that to happen? What's the next step?" Each question is designed to create space for the coachee to discover something, to move a step forward, and those particular questions can even be asked in that precise order. The rationale for these questions is described in the Developing Coaching Leadership section.

As a Coaching Leader, you want to be Aware of what team members aren't getting about themselves and their situation, so you can notice where you can make the biggest difference. In the

---

[30] At one point we considered calling it Connecting Leadership, because it connects people with their path, and connects all the forms of leadership. Like Journeying Leadership and Inspirational Leadership it sits on the Path that joins the Present with the Future.

short term, this means getting yourself out of the way.

Coaching Leaders have an Awareness of the forthcoming challenges that team members will face, whether or not they are yet aware of them.

You also want to get closer to what we call the "causal level". For example, someone in your team is suffering from stress: it may be caused by overwork, which may reflect a lack of delegation on their part driven by a lack of trust in others, which in turn reflects a lack of trust in themselves. Like all good coaches, as a Coaching Leader you want to work where you can make the biggest difference. Since they probably have plenty of evidence of their own ability to deliver, you could ask them how much evidence they need before they trust others to deliver, and go on to ask how much evidence they need before they really trust themselves to deliver.

In the pure coaching model, each person's answers for their work and life have a validity that no-one else's answers could ever have. However, in the context of what we call Coaching Leadership we include a range of leadership activities that aid development, including mentoring and the power of example.

As well as enabling greater individual performance, leaders are interested in enabling greater team performance. How do you get there? One aspect is to foster adult-to-adult[31] relations within the team, which you may model in your relationships.

Leaders are not only interested in where their Team is now, they are interested in the challenges that face the team as they move forward; the obstacles team members see along the path in front of them.

We describe the form that fits here as Coaching Leadership[32]. It connects team with potential team, and present with future.

---

[31] We reference adult-to-adult relationships and other aspects of the Transactional Analysis model within the context of Adult Leadership.

[32] Daniel Goleman and his co-authors' "New Leaders" recognizes coaching as one of a number of leadership styles. See the appendix: The New Leaders and 3-Dimensional Leadership.

Coaching Leaders enable others to succeed. They see themselves as part of the team, not someone who operates on it. They connect the team's hopes and fears, and enable them to get past hurdles, and clear obstacles out of the way. They understand that it is not "all about them", and that they cannot succeed on their own.

Inspirational Leadership

We inspire by showing people a greater version of themselves. The potential self they have not yet become.

We say that everyone is capable of greatness. Or, to state it in the negative, we make no presumption that people are not capable of greatness. Unfortunately, however, people often make that assumption for themselves.

While people may be reminded of the greatness in themselves by seeing greatness in others, including in their leader, they are also likely to say, that is just someone else being great. They could never be so.

Here we are, living in economies that offer a myriad of choices, in dynamic societies in which technology presents a stream of changes, writing off our own potential to be great. In many cases, the fear of being rejected by the team chokes off tentative leadership aspirations. Knowing not only that you can be great, but that everyone in your team can be great, or at least great at something, can be infectious.

One of our big challenges is we suppose we can't or won't be great. We stifle our potential, we settle for ourselves as we are. Inspirational Leaders change all that. When you find a great team, you have usually found an Inspirational Leader.

Inspirational Leaders believe in their team, they also believe in every team member. If not in the performance they are currently demonstrating then in their potential. They know that they don't know how great it can be, but they know it can be great. And this conviction is transmitted to the team members themselves, who transform their performance.

We may all be able to remember someone who believed in us, a teacher, a family member or a friend, someone who believed in us when we didn't. They gave us what we call the gift of belief, which made the difference. That was Inspiration Leadership.

As preparation for becoming a more Inspirational Leader, you may want to work through Self-Leadership, from Authentic Leadership through Journeying Leadership and Inspired Leadership, all of which puts you in a great place to lead others, including enabling them to sense their own potential.

Anyone can work with a team as it is, albeit more or less functionally. An Inspired Leader goes ahead of where the team is now to sense its latent talents and bring them to the fore. How does an Inspired Leader do this?

Start by becoming Aware that everyone is currently no more than a shadow of their future selves[33]: they have discovered a tiny proportion of their future potential. True, you may not know this for a fact, but you don't know the opposite either, so you might as well go with this more liberating assumption.

Look for their talents and potential talents. Give them space to perform. Expect – rather than demand – that little bit more: "Catch them doing things right".[34]

Why haven't others sensed their potential?. To some extent it is a matter of time. We accumulate knowledge and skills. It is also a matter of fear. Not aiming high reduces the risks of failure, and it is a common human trait to settle for average, providing as it does a strong likelihood of continued membership of the group, whether at work, socially or at home.

Inspirational Leaders make it feel OK to go further because they help you to discover that is who you really are[35]. They help us to become aware of and connect with our own potential. They help us to feel great about the person we can become. Consider for a moment your response to the question, "Who can you become?"

Inspired Leaders remind others of their greatness. Inspirational leaders take people out of themselves and into something greater. They take people into a version of their own future. As the Inspirational Leader causes you to sense more of your potential, you are inspired!

---

[33] We have inverted the traditional saying that someone is "a shadow of their former selves".

[34] See the One Minute Manager books by Kenneth Blanchard and Spencer Johnson.

[35] We may regard the future self as existing only in the future or as being included in the present self, like a flower that is yet to bloom.

Leading in the World

The purpose of leadership is to change the world, or some part of it. As well as being able to lead themselves and others, leaders look outward at the world they affect. We introduce three forms of Leading in the World:

– Grounded Leadership

– Challenging Leadership

– Visionary Leadership

And these three Forms of Leadership complete the tour.

Grounded Leadership

Grounded Leaders notice what already exists and what does not. They see the pieces, the overall picture, and what is missing. Think of it as another three-step.

We spend a lot of our time chasing shadows. Grounded Leaders see the shadows too but they also see the object that's blocking the light. They can work on moving the object, or brightening the light, or accessing an additional resource.

Grounded Leaders see things as they are and see beyond the world of forms. They think causally rather than casually. We say that the Grounded Leader is Aware of the world, deeply Connects with it and Transforms the world.

They know they don't see everything: they know there are always more perspectives, and they are likely to be interested in them. Right now you are receiving millions of bits of information visually, soundly and touchingly, but you are screening most of them out and bend most of the rest to fit your beliefs; it's what we all do.

So Grounded Leaders know there are always different ways of seeing things. They know they don't see the whole picture, at best a sketch, and only from an angle or two. Leaders are always working with a level of unknowingness. And knowing that you don't know frees you to learn. As soon as you think you know, you have lost it.

At the risk of getting a little bit deep, Grounded Leaders know that the way that they see the world is just the way that they see it; a lens is just a lens. To put it in rather more prosaic terms, no-one knows everything, the leader included.

While the Grounded Leader remains keen to gather information, they know there will never be enough, and a view is just a view. Leaders often act on gut feeling.

Awareness of the world is so much more than just noticing it. Because it includes acceptance that it is as it is: the present is accepted, and in the acceptance there in no judgment. There's no point fighting this moment; doing so would only deplete your energies. We've all met people who get worked up about the way things are "it's so bad!" without doing anything about it. Far from leading the situation, the situation has got them. Others deny that it is the way that it is: "But it shouldn't be like that!" Once you accept it, you can Connect with it, and then start to Transform it.

Because they see a sketch of the whole panorama, they can see what and where it isn't working. So Grounded Leaders are likely to take action. They can be subtle and they can be quite demanding.

Freed from the urge to judge, the Grounded Leader is open to more hypotheses. What's really going on here? What are the key factors? What options do we have, or could we have? And having been through something like that analysis there may be a "This shall not be" moment of decision. Or a skip to a Challenging Leader form where a decision is made to avoid an upcoming rock, or even a leap to a Vision of what can be.

There's a juxtaposition between Grounded and Visionary Leadership. The Grounded Leader works with things as they are, the Visionary with things as they could be, Grounded works with the current reality and the Visionary with future possibility. Neither has a complete picture. If the Visionary Leader has their head in the clouds, the Grounded Leader has their feet on the ground. Both are required.

Challenging Leadership

Challenging Leaders notice things that haven't yet happened; they sense challenges that lie in wait, they navigate the rapids that must be passed before the ocean is reached. At a maximum, they seize possibility, at a minimum their task is to keep the ship afloat: they sense both possibility and danger.

We like to think of the Challenging Leader navigating their way through the rapids of a fast-flowing river. They know there is a current, they know there are rocks, and they are going to do their best to avoid them. They know there is always a way forward, though it may be the least-bad way forward, and it may not take us quite where we want to be. But this they know: there is always a way.

They are also Aware that most problems are imaginary, we imagine the worst likely outcomes beforehand, and that can be really useful, because the solutions can also emerge in our imagination too.

Challenging Leaders' bottom line is survival. And they are born to survive. They don't give up, they are resourceful[36]. They are creative in the way they address issues, but most of all they're tenacious. When all around are losing their heads[37], Challenging Leaders keep theirs. They connect with the challenges that life invariably presents.

In the popular culture, the hero is the one who steps in and addresses the crisis, overcoming overwhelming odds to succeed. If heroic leadership is a form of leadership it sits here.

The Challenging Leaders' top line is making the most of circumstances. Knowing there is always a way ahead they're alive to opportunities and possibilities. They are Aware that life throws up surprises and they are pragmatic.

---

[36] We found it hard to capture this Form of Leadership in one word. At one stage, Resourceful Leaders was in the frame and then Heroic Leaders, which we might have gone for except for its heritage.

[37] Adapted from the original, "If you can keep your head when all about you are losing theirs and blaming it on you …, you'll be a man, my son!", Rudyard Kipling.

They are doubters: so-called good news is seldom as good as it looks, and bad news seldom as bad. It's all about what happens next.

They understand that the probable path between where you are and where you want to be is not a straight line; it's likely to be strewn with difficulties. And that is OK; that is what they are there for. They are Aware that most obstacles are imaginary or avoidable and most of the rest are temporary. Nothing gets in their way for too long.

They know tomorrow's world will be created, whatever it looks like. The future is unavoidable. The question is: what will it look like? They have the will to form that future.

Visionary Leadership

Unlike our Grounded Leaders, Visionaries see things as they aren't. They see what could be, even though it isn't yet there, and may never be, until and unless the Visionary Leader gets to work. Visionary Leaders see things in contrast[38].

You can be a Visionary Leader for your team, your family, your community; the same processes apply. Everyone can have a vision. Visions enable Transformation by giving you something to aim for. Think of a vision as being an amazing outcome, seen at a moment in time: a fulfilled team, an amazing product, a happy family. Though you get to choose what you envision, most people don't.

To a Visionary, the Future is as real as the present, even more real. Like Einstein, they spend much of their time in their imagination[39]. As you look at, and even sense the world, you may have a feeling. As a Visionary contemplates the Future, a feeling also emerges, and it may be more powerful. A sense of an absolute knowing that "this can be", which is not to say that it will, it's just one possible future.

Anything that isn't working as well as it could, needs Visionary Leadership: a team, a company, a family, a society.

Visionary Leadership is popular. When we ask people which Form of Leadership they would most like to develop, Visionary Leadership usually comes out on top. But it is poorly understood.

Visionary Leaders have to combine at least three different traits: first, they must be able to go into the future and see how things could be, that's the Awareness bit; second, they have to be able to know that it can be, the equivalent of having faith, which happens when they Connect with it; third, they have to be able to share the vision with others in a way that causes them to feel it can be and want to help make it so, which enables Transformation.

---

[38] Originally this read "in negative", to bring to mind the negative of a photograph, without conveying the popular sense of the negative word.

[39] According to Albert Einstein: "Your imagination is your preview of life's forthcoming attractions".

Let's look at each in turn.

How do they go into the Future? Even a visionary may admit that the future only ever exists in our imagination. But that is where we may meet it. In practice, we may visualize all kinds of things, including mutually exclusive outcomes, many of which never come to pass. Depending on how we best sense images, we may not see it so much as have a feeling about it. As with most things, practice makes perfect. And this is where the process starts.

In summary, Visionary Leadership sees what does not exist, connects with that vision and brings it into reality. What does not exist is much more interesting to the Visionary Leader than what does exist. They spend time in their imagination, trusting that what may be imagined may be turned into reality. But that imagination is grounded enough in the present to have validity for themselves and others. Without that grounding, they may be visionary, but they will be unable to lead as they will not be able to connect with the situation of those they wish to lead.

How do you create a vision? You can look around your world and see what doesn't work, but – and here's the magical part – rather than dwelling on it not working, simply imagine it working well: what does that look like? How does that make you feel? Do you notice something approaching desire? Noticing what does not work is a great jumping off point, but it is only the beginning. And whatever you do, don't continue to focus on what isn't working with an air of resignation or you will get stuck in the mud; flip the future.

One way out of rut-like thinking is to notice that everything changes. The way it is now is not the way it will be. You may as well detach yourself from it because like everything else it is temporary. Given that change is inevitable, you may as well make your choices. It is something like seeing in contrast.

A Visionary Leader sees what does not exist. They are ahead of the curve. They don't so much see the future as a preferred version of it.

When you become Aware of this possibility, it is very important to nurture it carefully. Be cautious who you expose it to, since many people unthinkingly snuff out new ideas.

How great a Visionary Leader would you like to become? Visionary Leaders know there's no-one to stop them, except themselves. And it is the smallness of our vision that holds most of us back.

A Preliminary 3-Dimensional Profile

Profiling can prompt self-awareness and aid your development[40]. Unfortunately it is sometimes used to put people in boxes, not least by the people who complete the profiles themselves! For these reasons we have developed a simple diagnostic.

It is a simple and personal ranking. It won't tell you that you are a better or worse leader than someone else. Great leaders are really only interested in how they – and others – can get better; not in who is supposed to be better than who. The profile will provide some sense of where you are already strong and where you can get better.

	Now	Path	Future
World	Grounded Leadership	Challenging Leadership	Visionary Leadership
Team	Adult Leadership	Coaching Leadership	Inspiring Leadership
Self	Authentic Leadership	Journeying Leadership	Inspired Leadership

Having reviewed the 9 Forms of Leadership, you can create your own 3-Dimensional Profile. Stage one is to identify the three Forms of Leadership that you believe are your:

Strongest
Weakest

The remaining three Forms will be your 'middle ground'.

---

[40] We think it can also help to shape leadership teams. A leadership team with strengths in a range of areas may be stronger than one in which the strengths are focused in one or two areas.

Placing three in each category will cover all 9 Forms of Leadership. In Stage two you are invited, for each of the above three categories, to select your strongest, your middle and your weakest Form of Leadership within each of the above three categories, subdividing each of them, so that all 9 are now in order. Take your time. Go back and review any of the Forms of Leadership that aren't so clear to you. Leaders trust their own judgment. How do you stack up? As you think about your behavior, what is your evidence for your relative capabilities?

For example, what is your evidence that you do Visionary Leadership?

	Evidence for your relative capability	
Visionary		
Challenging		
Grounded		
Inspirational		
Coaching		
Adult		
Inspired		
Journeying		
Self		

Having assessed the evidence, what score would you give yourself out of ten for each of the capabilities? By all means write in the right hand column. Which, if any, of your capabilities are changing in order? And looking ahead, what would be different if you developed your behavior by 2 marks out of ten on each capability?

	Different behaviour two marks higher	
Visionary		
Challenging		
Grounded		
Inspirational		
Coaching		
Adult		
Inspired		
Journeying		
Self		

And what will your behaviour look like at each of these higher levels? If you were to pick a priority Leadership Form to develop, which is it? And so we turn to 3-Dimensional leadership development.

3-DIMENSIONAL LEADERSHIP DEVELOPMENT

3-Dimensional Leadership Development

You may already have some clues about your own development.

We don't think leadership development is a one-off activity; we believe it is a lifelong pursuit as described in Journeying Leadership. Still, there may be phases in your life when you make a big leap forward, when you see things afresh, and this may be one of them.

We invite you to suppose you can develop all 9 Forms of Leadership, and of course we have no basis for supposing that you can't do so. You may feel you are relatively gifted in some Forms of Leadership and weaker in others. Others may see you differently. Your priority won't necessarily be to develop your weakest areas – though it could be – you may want to become utterly brilliant in your strongest area.

As well as working on the 9 Forms of Leadership, we can work in a cross-cutting way, for example on Awareness, Connection and Transformation, which may make a difference in a range of Forms, and it is to them that we initially turn.

As a leader you can develop your capabilities across the board. For example, you can work on self-awareness[41], both your current self (bottom left), your future vision for yourself (bottom right) and your development path (bottom middle), that's a left to right move.

You can work on your connection with future possibilities for self, team and world, a bottom to top move through the right hand column, etc. We'll explore future possibilities later when you have discovered more about the kind of leader you are and the leadership you want to develop.

---

[41] Self-Awareness is a well-established term in Emotional Intelligence. However, we add awareness of future self, and the path to it.
For more, view the appendix on Emotional Intelligence and 3D Leadership.

Developing Your Ability to ACT

Awareness, Connection and Transformation inform your leadership and permeate each of the 9 Forms of Leadership. Before we review them, let's start with something that often gets in the way.

The F before the ACT

Where present, fear prevents transformation. And we remain hard-wired to notice threats before we notice opportunities. However, fear tends to push us into a "fight or flight" mindset where creative and transformational possibilities are closed off.

But think about it for a minute: What is fear? And given that everyone is different, how do you experience it? What if you thought of a fear as a fragment of your personality – an inner child – that needs reassurance, or even as a messenger that needs to be acknowledged before it will move on. In many leadership cultures, we pretend that fears are not present – they become unspeakable – and we tend to suppress rather than address them. Could you befriend and even master your own inner fears? Developing Awareness, Connection and Transformation of your fears will enable your development as a leader.

Developing Awareness

As you read these words, what are you aware of? If you are reading a printed version, you may now be aware of the ink on the page, the texture of the page perhaps, and your hand holding the book. Internally, you may be aware of the flow of thoughts in your mind, your emotions, your hopes and fears, and even what is happening in your gut. Interesting how things move into and out of your Awareness. Moving beyond yourself, you may be aware of others, of the current situation, of possibilities.

You can walk into a room and become aware of the human dynamics. Or you can walk into a room and notice none of them. Anyone can be more or less aware in any situation. Developing Awareness is a habit.

Of course, you can't focus on a myriad of things simultaneously, and you don't need to. But like a jig-saw player who momentarily directs their full attention on one piece, leaders may be aware of the wider picture. One of our clients, for example, makes sure that he invests at least two hours a week becoming more aware of what is happening in his company's wider environment. The more aware you become, the bigger the difference you can make. You are invited to become super-aware.

What impedes the development of Awareness? First, we suggest a lack of Awareness that Awareness can be developed! Second, we propose a preference for the familiar over the unfamiliar and the comfort zone over the stretch zone. In other words, fear.

Developing Connection

As we have said, Awareness is the gateway to Connection. For our part, we love connecting: ourselves with purpose, problems with solutions, and people with one another. A great connector is, in this context, like a cook who is able to turn a number of separate ingredients into a feast. And the more you practice connecting, the more skilled a connector you become. You immediately know what works with what, how to throw things together, in fact you don't need to think about it for a moment, it has become part of who you are.

Just as the leader, team and world are connected to themselves and one another, the present, future and path from one to the other are equally connected, and Connection unites Awareness and Transformation. The point is: Connection is real; the only question is: what form will it take?

As we have already proposed, fear would be an impediment to Connection too. "What would she think? What if he rejects my idea? What if they don't get on?" These speculative and usually unanswered thoughts tend to stifle Connection. One antidote is to answer them: She may not get it, he may not buy my idea, and they may not get on, but what if she does, he does and they do?

Connection is vital both within each form and between forms: the present with the future, the leader with the team, the team with the mission and so on. From a leader's point of view, nothing happens without Connection.

Notice where you are holding back from connecting: the more honest you can be the better. And notice why you are holding back. Be as specific as you can and be OK about whatever comes up. Almost certainly, you are encountering your imagination, positive or negative.

Developing Transformation

Managers optimize, leaders transform. So how can you develop your own ability to enable Transformation?

It turns out that there is an Awareness, Connection, Transformation process for developing transformational capability. Having already become Aware that you, the team, the world are the way they are, and of course that our future speculations are as they are, notice that all forms are subject to change.

Consequently, the form that anything takes is temporary. We could also imagine a continuance of something. Take yourself: you are very different to the person you were when you were, say, 10 years old, but arguably there is a sense in which you remain you; the essential you[42]. The same applies to teams, organizations, and the world we affect, only more obviously so. Still, form changes[43]. And over time, and with the benefit of Awareness and Connection, transformation is likely. Almost everything is progressing or regressing.

The first key, then, is not to be attached to the present Form. It's just one shape that whatever it is happens to be taking at the moment. It can and will disappear. Holding on to the present

---

[42] We like to talk about the "continuing self", as a label for whatever aspects of the self may remain.

[43] As has been said, all modern philosophy is mere footnotes to Plato, and this viewpoint of course echoes Plato's Theory of Forms.

prevents the future: leaders let the present go so that it may be replaced by something greater. To echo Plato again, everything is but a shadow of its potential, and leaders really are in the business of realizing potential[44].

A second key is to know that Transformation is always possible. Actually, everyone wants things to be better, though they may think it won't happen, or something untoward will happen along the way, and so on. Moreover, in principle every member of your team wants to contribute to making things better, just as you do, though they may think that they can't or that their contribution would not be welcome. The leader knows there is a better way of being in the present, a better path, and a better future, and isn't defensive about the fact that we haven't found it yet!

A third key is not to get in the way, not to stymie it. Most parts of the world have evolved culturally and physically even in the past fifty years. And individuals, teams and organizations can shift much more quickly.

---

[44] We've heard people say "We enable people to realise their potential". You may enable people to realise some of their potential, or at least to realise that it exists, but you will never enable them to realise all of it: it's unknowable.

A Little Reflection

You can sense your own inclination to be Aware, Connect and Transform at each level by scoring yourself 0-10 in the following table where 0 means nothing is happening, 5 is average and 10 is perfect. We invite you to trust your intuition and see what comes up:

	Aware	Connect	Transform	Totals
World				
Team				
Self				
Totals				

If you wanted to improve just one of those spaces, which one would come to mind, and what difference would that make?

Now we turn to how you may develop each of the Forms of Leadership.

Authentic Leadership Development

Authenticity is the work of a lifetime. But as it is said, the rest of your life starts here. And if one could only choose one Form of Leadership to develop, it is hard not to pick Authentic Leadership, because it informs all of the other Forms. We offer a number of practices you can use to help you develop your Authentic Leadership.

Your values

Get to know your values. Only you can make the selection and there is no right or wrong about them. So what is really important to you? You could start by making a list of words that convey something important to you[45].

Get as many as you can and then pick a top ten. Write them down on a sheet with a couple of columns to their right. Answer these questions for each of your values: Why is it important to you? If we were to follow you around during the last week, how would we see you living each value?

Your beliefs

We all have beliefs about ourselves, others and the world. And most of them we picked up from other people! Start by becoming more aware of your beliefs about yourself. Ask yourself this question: what do you deeply believe about yourself? You may find mutually exclusive ideas come to mind: for example that you are brilliant and that you are inadequate! Most of us approach this exercise in a state of trepidation, just notice that and explore: only you can know you.

For each of the principal beliefs you have clarified: What is your evidence for that belief?[46] If you were going to review the evidence for the opposite belief, what would come to mind?

---

[45] There's a values list in the Appendix: Leadership Values; but you might prefer to start by making your own list.
[46] This is a handy question often used in Cognitive Behavioural Therapy (CBT) which helps to highlight how unfounded our beliefs may be.

Your behaviours

Starting with this month, find fifteen minutes a day to write about your day. No editing, just write and see what comes up. Describe the principal events of the day and how you responded to them. Notice where you were inspired and where you were foolish: own up to yourself.

Notice your intention for the day and where you were on and off track. Don't beat yourself up, just describe what happened and broadly how you feel about it. There's no need to review what you have written – though it can be fun – the process of writing is itself a review of the day.

This practice of keeping a journal is not so easy for people who like to see immediate measurable progress, but life isn't always like that. On the plus side your self-awareness will expand within a month.

Your acceptance

Logically, you know you are you. You've got no-one else. Everyone is imperfect, everyone has issues and challenges.

From an authenticity point of view, the challenge is to realise that you are who you are and that's OK. A practice as simple as saying to yourself that "I accept myself for who I am" helps some people. Whatever talents you have are yours to use, whatever talents you don't have are not a burden!

Journeying Leadership Development

You are currently developing yourself as a Journeying Leader. Reading this book is such a development activity. Developing your Journeying Leadership is informed by Authentic Leadership[47] – they are both aspects of Self-Leadership – but Journeying Leaders travel much further.

Challenge

What is the biggest challenge you have successfully overcome in your life? What was the situation, how did you respond to it, and what difference has that made to who you are now?

Review

What are your biggest successes in your life so far? What are your biggest failures – or if you prefer – surprising outcomes? What was present that enabled the successes to happen? And what was not there that would have prevented the failures?

Journeying

Journeying Leaders know they are on a journey: so what does yours look like? Write the story of your life to date – if you like, start with your professional life – in 500 words[48]. Notice key external events and your responses to them, the initiatives you took and the results, what worked as you expected and what did not. Who else can make sense of your life? Having written the story to date, write the continuing story of your professional life. Choose to make it a great story. One in which you accomplish whatever it is that you want to accomplish, noticing how you develop in the process.

---

[47] We recommend you review the section on Authentic Leadership before viewing this section.
[48] It's an arbitrary number you are free to vary but a framework often helps.

One thing

By its nature, Journeying Leadership is concerned with the development of all leadership capabilities.

So if you were going to do one thing to vastly improve the quality of your leadership, what would that be? Trust your response. And once you've captured it: what difference will it make to you? And once it's clear: what has to happen for it to happen? What did you believe when you were 18 years old, about yourself and about the world? What do you believe now? And now for the fun bit, what might you believe in ten years' time?

	18 year old belief	Current belief	Belief in ten year's time
The World			
Myself			

What patterns can you see, and what happens as you roll the tape forward into the future?

Overview

If you review your professional development, your career, your life as a whole, how would you feel about it? What comes up if you were to write a summary of the story of your life in 100 words? And what's the gist when you edit that down to a dozen words? And how do you feel about that?

Planning

Create your own leadership development plan. What behaviours are you going to change? What results will that give you? And what difference will that make to you?

Inspired Leadership Development

Only you can develop yourself as an Inspired Leader. Developing your Authentic Leadership and your Journeying Leadership provides a base for developing Inspired Leadership.

Sources

When have you been at your most inspired? What was it that caused you to be inspired, and what in general inspires you? The lives of other leaders, great solutions to taxing problems, what really makes you inspired? It could be big or little, near or far, unusual or commonplace.

Ideal

What does your ideal you look like? What do you have to know about yourself in order to feel really inspired?

What is your sense of a good life well lived? How can you visualize it – when you close your eyes how well can you start to see it – and once you see it, what does that feel like? Your answers to these questions are really important. In fact, they have the power to determine your future.

Brilliance

Get really clear on what you are really good at[49] and aim to become brilliant in at least one of those areas. Make really clear to yourself your intention to be brilliant at it. We all have brilliance within us, but most of us aren't even trying to be brilliant, just settling for membership of the pack.

Imagination

When you see yourself as an amazing leader, what do you see? Let yourself actually visualise yourself being that leader: how

---

[49] Strengthsfinder is one such development tool we recommend.

do you walk, how do you talk? Spend time in your imagination; Inspired Leaders do.

Mission

We talked about mission in the main narrative: what's yours? Spend time with this and don't be vexed if nothing comes to mind immediately; this is serious work. At the risk of getting lucky, imagine you have just completed your life's work: what have you done, what comes to mind now? The mission you may not have chosen for yourself. If you do have a mission what would it be?[50]

---

[50] As we remarked in the main text, you aren't limited to one mission - you can have lots, e.g. a professional mission, a personal mission and so on, though they may be consistent with one another, and each mission can have several parts.

Adult Leadership Development

There are many ways you can develop your Adult Leadership. And of course, becoming more comfortable as an Authentic Leader, is a good start.

Listen

Leaders listen. Where do your followers want more direction? Where do they want more flexibility and freedom? How do they want to be led by you? How do they experience the relationship and how would they like it to be different? What really helps their performance and what sometimes impedes it? Notice if you feel threatened in any way. If you do, they are likely to sense it and clam up. You don't have to challenge any of it or immediately commit to any of it: just thank them for it, take it on board, and reflect. Later, you can come to a view.

Getting feedback from your team members and colleagues can be quite easy and informal. You don't need to ask them to judge you, though they may imagine that is the risk.

For example, ask them for one thing you do that really helps them in their work. And then ask them for one thing they would like you to do more of. You don't have to agree or disagree, you just want to be more aware.

Initially, they may try to give you the answer they think you want, which is of course no good to you at all! If and when they sense that you really want to learn, and that it is safe to give feedback, they will do so, and you understand more. Also, your relationship with them will become more adult-to-adult.

Awareness

Become aware of moments when you tend to feel defensive and go into a controlling or submissive state. When do you remember doing that? What has tended to cause you to be defensive? What's the underlying fear? What did you imagine would happen if you did not take control or submit? Did you see it as a competition?

Notice what tends to put you into a childlike state, one where you give up. Remember when it has most recently occurred: what went on? And notice what has tended to put you into a controlling parent place too.

Appreciation

Develop your appreciation of others, especially team members. What positive qualities have you noticed recently in your colleagues, and what have you done to reinforce them[51]?

---

[51] Above all, people value attention and will go out of their way to give you more of whatever gets your attention.

Coaching Leadership Development

Everyone else is on a journey too whether they know it or not. And it's a great responsibility to enable them to find their way forward. It is one thing to help them on their journey, even better is to help them to sense the answer themselves, which is what Coaching Leaders do.

The principal tool Coaching Leaders use is of course coaching. And coaching is easy to do. Unfortunately, it is also so easy to do badly! One of the keys is to know that you simply don't know: you don't know the answer and you definitely don't know what their answer would be, so you are going to create some room for them to discover it.

To keep it simple, we have discovered some powerful questions that help in most coaching conversations. Even on their own they enable some progress to be made. For example:

What would you like to be different? (An important starting point because people will otherwise often spend time telling you how things are not the way they want them to be. You want to point them in the direction of a solution right away so that they start to become Aware of it.)

What will that look like? (This is a natural follow-on question that prompts people to start to visualize a potential solution, the beginning of the Connection process.)

How will that make you feel? (This question helps people to Connect with an outcome through their feelings. Usually, they will feel quite good just through imagining a solution.)

Why is that important to you? (Now you start to probe the underlying rationale, which is usually not obvious to the coachee.)

What has to happen for that to happen? (We have employed this sentence hundreds of times and it usually prompts a powerful response. No-one is put off by the repetition, which effectively makes it a command to the unconscious.)

What resource do you need to get a great result? (You can skip this question if it doesn't seem necessary.) An ideal response would be: I don't need any resource!

What first step comes to mind? (An obvious question but effective none the less.)

When an unusual word is offered, like "free" or "trapped", "stress" or whatever, simply ask: "Free, what is that?" which allows the coachee to understand what they mean by what they have said, it peels back a layer. Notice that we absolutely don't say "What do you mean by X?" as it tends to encourage people to find the "right" dictionary answer, rather than what they mean.

Try asking some or all of those questions the next time someone comes up with a problem that they wouldn't mind dumping on your desk. You may pleased by how they take responsibility for moving it forward.

Look for opportunities to coach respectfully, and you will find them everywhere.

Inspirational Leadership Development

Spotting others' talents – i.e. becoming Aware of them – can become habit-forming! Nurturing them, in other words Connecting with them to enable Transformation can be hugely rewarding. It will also mean you develop a greater team.

Brilliance at work

Here's a practical exercise. Make a note of the names or initials of a handful of members of your team. They can be people who report to you and work alongside and even someone to whom you report; think of them all as being on your team. Now let something come to mind that each of them already is or could become brilliant at.

How do you know what they could become brilliant at it? You don't! And they probably don't either, and that's the point. At the same time, you don't know there's nothing they could become brilliant at, you are helping to identify a talent that could be developed, a space that can be explored.

Realising Potential

When you are working one-to-one with their team, try to Connect more deeply with their future potential. How do you do that? Start by imagining they are brilliant. It doesn't have to be specific. They will almost immediately start to pick up your belief in them. You are giving them a little more encouragement to discover how good they can be.

Respect

Cultivate a respect for your team members that borders on the reverential. They are, after all, your fellow human beings. As you show them greater respect – which you are really directing to the potential they have yet to manifest – they will respond.

The Inspirational Leader helps them to find it, then nurtures the capability and sets them flying. How do you do that?

Language

Notice your language towards each of your team members. How would you describe the relationship? How free do you think they feel to really engage with their work? Where may you be getting in their way? And, of course, you could always ask them.

Grounded Leadership Development

Look around your world: what's working brilliantly? What isn't working at all? What really isn't the way you feel it should be?

What is happening for yourself, your team, and the community you affect? How do they see what is happening for them?

Focusing on these questions, write a Journal of a day at work in which you notice what you notice about the world around you. Also describe any emotional reaction you have to them. Your responses - emotional and mental - to the world you perceive are also a part of your world and it is important that you recognize and accept them for what they are, because you want to get past your reaction to Connect with what is really there.

Awareness

Regularly practice noticing your feet on the ground, the air on your face, what you see around you. Notice your breathing and use these sensations to connect with the present moment. Notice what you have not been noticing. Get a great external focus. Practice connecting with the world around you. What do you really love, what makes you feel great, and what doesn't? It's OK either way, you just want to know. You want the data.

Routine

Create a daily routine where you really do notice what is happening in the world around you. Try to do so without letting yourself get excited or depressed; just notice it and keep a steady head. Notice the patterns you can see.

Rating the world

Select a number of aspects of your world and score them from 0-10. For example, your work life, your family life, your social life, and notice which is the highest and which the lowest.

Notice your response as you consider doing such a thing: uncomfortable, don't want to go there, or ready to face it? What would it look like if you improved each of them by one or two numbers, so for example, a 6 becomes an 8?

These are all exercises designed to make you more attentive.

Challenging Leadership Development

What are the biggest leadership challenges you have overcome to date? Make a note of the three that first come to mind, and briefly describe what happened and how you responded? Looking at what you have written: what have you learnt about yourself as a leader; what impact has each of them had on the person you are now?

Notice what sometimes goes wrong. What happened and what was the cause? What did you miss and what could you have picked up earlier? If your experience is like that of others[52], there'll be some positives, in fact the overall balance may well be positive. If this is true, how much sense does it make to label one experience good and another bad. You simply don't know, but you do know that you have to get on with it.

Can you remember one where you held back, where you fluffed it? What was your experience? What held you back – if you were afraid of something, what was it? What did you not know, the knowing of which may have produced a different outcome?

Looking forwards, you can practice assessing situations together with the biggest challenges that you foresee, and how you can best pre-empt or mitigate them.

We propose that Challenging Leaders stay calm even in a crisis. The next time things get tough, practice low breathing. Better still, practice it now! Learn about diaphragmatic breathing and the effect that it has on your nervous system. When you breathe low, you get calm.

Notice how your Awareness changes in a crisis: if you step into a "fight or flight" mode your Awareness will become more limited. Notice when you get wound up and unwind. Practice peripheral vision: it will help you to see what you haven't been seeing.

---

[52] Confronting a number of difficulties some years ago, a wise man said to one of the authors, "You are facing a crisis", "Yes, that's it!" I immediately agreed. "Good", he said. "What do you mean good?" "In a crisis you have to grow". But the smart thing is to grow without waiting for the crisis.

Remember, as we have remarked, that there is always a way forward, even if it may be a least-painful way forward; and as well as the options we have already identified, there will almost certainly be more for us to find.

Visionary Leadership Development

What does your front door look like? Got it? OK, you can visualize. Many of us are doing it much of the time. We see ourselves missing a bus, making a call, catching a train, and having lunch; in each case we do it before it happens. It's that easy, now the question is what to focus upon?

What do you see?

Make a list of three things you would like to be different in your home life, your work life, your team, and the results you get? Let them come to mind without judging any of them, in other words become Aware of them as possibilities. Once you have completed this short list, start to visualize them as though they are already complete. Imagine yourself in a space with it completed; this is a way of letting your unconscious know this is a result that you want to accomplish.

Feeling too

As you visualize, Connect with how you feel. If it is a positive feeling, notice its location and let it grow: is it in your head, heart or gut? If you have never done this before, you are in for some fun. If the feeling has shade, what shade comes to mind? If it has a shape, what shape does it have? If it is a negative feeling think of something else!

Like a movie

Think of a project on which you may already be working and run a similar process. Visualize a positive outcome and then run a film in your imagination of the key events from the start to that outcome.

Connect with it and allow that possible future to affect the way you feel right now.

Mission

Your will want your vision to be consistent with your mission if you have identified one. Imagine a scene that represents the accomplishment of your mission, or some major milestone. If you haven't identified a mission, it may help to do so.

Think big

Let's try something even bigger. If you could change one thing in the world what comes to mind? Give yourself some time. What is the biggest contribution you would like to make?

Or ask yourself this: If you could accomplish any one thing, and you knew you could not fail, what would that one thing be? Give yourself time with this too. We are so often reminded of the way things are, by for example the media and our surroundings, we completely forget how wonderful they could be. Visionary Leaders remind themselves of their vision. In the popular vernacular, it's what gets them out of bed in the morning.

Future flipping

Look at the world you can affect and notice what isn't working so well. Got something? Now imagine it working really well. What does that look like, what do you see happening?

Year

Imagine a wonderful end of year outcome. What would you most like to see? Now consider whether you are serious about that. If you are really serious, see it happening and play the tape of it emerging in your mind. We don't see this as a guarantee, but it will give you some momentum.

You and Your Leadership Journey

No-one can make you lead. We say no-one can make you a leader, except you.

We agree with those who say becoming a leader is not about remembering which techniques to use, helpful as they may be. You don't "do" being a leader. Authentic Leaders and Inspirational Leaders are being themselves. It's a matter of who you have become.

You can live each Form of Leadership your way. We suggest you are here to express who you are, to work with and through others and to make a difference, and that is what leaders do.

May we wish you good luck on your leadership journey.

Appendices

Appendix

Lines of Leadership

Those who are interested may wish to reflect further upon the model through this linear review. In each dimension are three "Lines of Leadership".

Within the Spatial dimension are:

Line 1: Self-Leadership
Line 2: Leading Team
Line 3: Leading a world

Within the Temporal dimension are:

Line 4: Leading in the Present
Line 5: Leading along the Path
Line 6: Leading into Future

And within the Being dimension are:

Line 7: Leading with Awareness
Line 8: Leading with Connection
Line 9: Leading Transformation

We start with three horizontal lines, the first of which is Self-Leadership.

Line 1: Self Leadership

As we have asserted, all leadership begins with leadership of the self. If you cannot lead yourself you cannot lead others. This is the territory of self-awareness and self-regard, of knowing oneself and one's capabilities, and sending one's potential. So the first three Forms of Leadership are all forms of Self-leadership.

Authentic Leadership	Journeying Leadership	Inspired Leadership

You may remember leaders who led by example, others who did not, and the difference that made to you[53]. When you lead yourself you lead by example, you walk your talk. Example is a leader's currency. Leaders who don't set an example don't lead.

Line 2: Leading Team

Leaders do not work alone. They work through others, usually a team. And the others may be a family, a small team, an organization, or a whole society; whichever, it's still leadership.

Leaders who maximize the performance and potential of the team will be much more effective that those who do not, however many hours they work.

Adult Leadership	Coaching Leadership	Inspirational Leadership

If you've worked with a leader who didn't care for team, you will remember the impact that had on your colleagues. Leaders who are unable to work well with others are unable to lead well. They may have the position, but at a deeper level they aren't getting it. In the Line of Leading Others there are three Forms of Leadership.

To put it bluntly, teams don't need leaders that don't serve their team[54]. So this is Line Two: it's interpersonal.

Line 3: Leading in the World

Leadership is purposeful. Leaders work with teams to affect something beyond them both, an outer community, a set of circumstances or world. The leaders and the team must reach

---

[53] "Becoming a leader is synonymous with becoming yourself." On Becoming a Leader, Warren Bennis.
[54] In times gone by, we had no choice. A medieval king or lord could command our allegiance, as could the only employer in town. Now, we can and do lead the leader who does not serve us.

beyond themselves or they have accomplished nothing[55].

This is Line Three: where end-results happen and where purpose resides. We all influence – or have the power to – our surroundings and beyond. And leaders look outward at that world, the "World we affect". Like the butterfly flapping its wings in the Sahara, our potential effects are vast. Three Forms of Leadership reside here:

| Grounded Leadership | Challenging Leadership | Visionary Leadership |

Again to put it bluntly, the world does not need leaders that are not interested in the well-being of the world they affect. In this context, win-lose is where the world loses.

So this spatial dimension has a rhythm: Leaders work on themselves, through their team to affect something beyond them. Now it is time to introduce another dimension.

We turn to three temporal Lines of Leadership each of which is represented by a column on our map of leadership:

Line 4: Leading in the Present

The temporal dimension presents three lines of leadership: the present, the path and the future. We start with the present moment: the great and glorious now[56].

| Authentic Leadership | Adult Leadership | Grounded Leadership |

Viewed philosophically, the present moment is the only time when anything ever actually happens. And from a leadership

---

[55] This may seem obvious, but many teams get absorbed in themselves and their organisation, or even their part of it, losing site of a wider purpose.

[56] As represented in the catchphrase "Being here now".

Appendix

perspective it is indeed the space from which everything happens, which takes us into the future.

We can start to look at two of the dimensions together: time and space. In this moment, the leader is interested in what is going on for herself, what is going on for others, and what is going on for the wider world.

They don't leave themselves out of the picture, or the team, and they don't neglect the world either. If, as a leader, you can't connect with the present moment, things look dicey.

This is harder than it may seem. How much of our reflection concerns fantasies we are having rather than realities?

If the present moment is fleeting, where do we go to next?

Line 5: Leading along the Path

As well as being here now, leaders sense the way forward, the upcoming path, the what is just around the corner.

| Journeying Leadership | Coaching Leadership | Challenging Leadership |

In a fast-changing world, it isn't possible to stay where we are. Preserving the present is seldom a viable option. We need to move forward even to stand still.

From the leaders' perspective, this requirement for continuing development applies to the leader, the team and the world. So we are on multiple paths, but before we can set off, we must first go into the future.

Line 6: Leading into the Future

Leaders usher in the future. If they aren't in the business of creating a future, they aren't leading.

| Grounded Leadership | Challenging Leadership | Visionary Leadership |

Appendix

What can we say about the future? There's a future for self, a future for team and a future for your world. At each level we are talking about aspects of what doesn't yet exist.

We can imagine potential of self, team and world. This is the territory of being inspired and inspiring others, and of Visionary Leadership. Without going into the future, it is impossible to see the upcoming path or even to know which fork in the road to take. So it often makes sense to go into "Time Three" in order to make sense of "Time Two".

Now we have looked at two dimensions, space and time, we come to the cross-cutting dimension in which leaders ACT.

Line 7: Awareness

Awareness underpins all 9 Forms of Leadership. While we call it a Line of Leadership for the sake of consistency, it is more like a level that permeates every Form of Leadership.

Aware of the Ground	Aware of the Challenges	Aware of the Vision
Aware of the Team	Aware of the Team's Challenges	Aware of the Team's Potential
Aware of the Self	Aware of the Journey	Aware of the Self's Potential

It includes awareness at all three Levels: so we have Awareness of Self[57], Awareness of Team, and Awareness of the world we affect.

We can immediately see that a leader who was not aware of these dimensions would be in some difficulty.

---

[57] Self-awareness and awareness of others are key building blocks of Emotional Intelligence. Awareness of the world we affect takes this further.

Appendix

In fact, we can be Aware of the present moment, future possibilities and a path between them.

In the present moment, Awareness means seeing it as it is. And once we are really aware that something is as it is, we can stop resisting or judging it, and move on. Awareness provides the foundation for everything that follows.

And in practice you can't Connect with what you are not Aware. Once you are Aware of it, Connection becomes possible, even likely.

Line 8: Connection

Connects with the Ground	Connects with the Challenges	Connects with the Vision
Connects with the Team	Connects with the Team's Challenges	Connects with the Team's Potential
Connects with the Self	Connects with the Journey	Connects with the Self's Potential

Leaders connect through all 9 Forms of Leadership. You know how it is when you really connect with someone; it's much more than being aware of them. When you really connect with the Team, they get who you are.

You can deeply connect with who you are, so that you really get yourself, you get what you are about, and everything slots into place.

You can connect with a vision of a future possibility, so that it starts to feel all but inevitable. You have a feeling of certainty that you are moving towards it; what some may describe as faith. Similarly, you can connect with others' potential, so that they begin to feel it too.

As you stay connected, the next phase naturally emerges.

Line 9: Transformation

Line 9 is Transformation: leaders know that form evolves.

Transforms the Ground	Transforms Challenges	Transforms the Vision
Transforms the Team	Transforms the Team's Challenges	Transforms Team Potential
Transforms the Self	Transforms the Journey	Transforms the Self's Potential

Leaders transform: achieving targets, maintaining margins, growing volumes, are all management activities. Transformation changes everything, or at least it changes something that affects everything. We say that Transformation has occurred when:

There is a new space, an expansion in one's perception that provides a new relationship to one or more of self, team and world.

Consequently, there are new perspectives and understandings. There's also a sense of increased harmony and connections (inner and outer)

Something new, beyond the old conception of the self and its original intentions, emerges.

In practice, we can then expect others' responses to recognize that there has been a profound change.

Appendix

Bibliography

Participants in our programmes often ask for pointers towards other books about leadership. Here are a few:

Becoming a Leader, Warren Bennis, published by Addison Wesley, 1989.

Leading Change, John P. Kotter, published by Harvard Review Press, 1996.

The 5 Dysfunctions of a Team, Patrick Lencioni, Manga Edition published Jossey-Bass, 2002.

The Seven Habits of Highly Effective People, Stephen Covey published by the Free Press in 1989.

The New Leaders, Daniel Goleman, Richard Boyatzis and Annie McKee, Little Brown, 2002. In the US published at Primal Leadership.

Building a Values-Driven Organisation, by Richard Barrett, published by Butterworth-Heinneman, 2006

"*The One Minute Manager*" books by Kenneth Blanchard and Spencer Johnson.

Appendix

Leadership and Time Management

Leaders sometimes say they're too busy for leadership development. We ask, "Well if you are all so busy doing all that stuff, who is leading the firm?" Time management continues to be a challenge.

So let's be clear: leaders lead, they don't do. Anyone can do things. Anyone can fill their diary with tasks, and feel in demand.

Without discipline, your schedule will get filled by others. And urgent activities tend to displace non-urgent ones.

	Urgent	Not-urgent
Important	Q1 Fires!	Q2 Almost all leadership activities
Not important	Q3	Q4

The 2-by-2 time management matrix [58]

However, almost all leadership activities are in Q2: Looking around at what is going on in the world, identifying upcoming challenges before they hit the firm, and developing a vision, are all non-urgent. To make more time available: delegate Q3 and Q1 work so you can get into Q2 and stay there for some part of most days.

---

[58] We first came across this in "First Things First" by Stephen Covey, A. Roger and Rebecca R. Merrill.

Appendix

Liberating Leadership

Leadership development is hindered by a history of limited thinking. Let us demolish some of it:

"Leaders are born, not made". You've heard this before, but how does anyone know it to be true? In fact, there are plenty of examples of people who become leaders. Anyone can lead. How you lead is more interesting[59].

"Leadership derives from title". In medieval times it did. As a serf you had no room to move, as a free man a little, even as a Knight you had to report to your Lord. These days, leaders discover themselves. They decide to become leaders!

"Leadership is only for the directors". With fast-changing information, decision-making and leadership must be distributed and local.

"Leadership is for them, it's not for you". We are all leaders now: with colleagues and in our wider lives. We are free to lead.

"Leadership is about winning": Leaders serve their teams, and together they serve the world they affect. Serving isn't winning. Leaders know we are in this together. Leaders compete but only with themselves.

---

[59] In Warren Bennis' view, "The most dangerous leadership myth is that leaders are born-that there is a genetic factor to leadership. This myth asserts that people simply either have certain charismatic qualities or not. That's nonsense; in fact, the opposite is true. Leaders are made rather than born".

Appendix

3D Leadership and Emotional Intelligence

A consultant once said Emotional Intelligence is leadership. We agree that Emotionally Intelligent leaders are much more likely to be effective. But we say there is much more to leadership.

Emotional Intelligence focuses on self-awareness and self-regard which provide the bases for self-management, and awareness of others and regard for others, which provide a base for management of others.

How does this relate to the 3D model? We place self-awareness, self-regard and self-management in Authentic Leadership. We then place an awareness of others, regard for others and management of others in Adult Leadership. However, the 3D Leadership Model also encompasses:

1. Connection and Transformation, which could also be fitted into Authentic and Adult Leadership.
2. The Path and the Future: EI tends to focus on the Now, while we say leaders have an equally strong focus on the future, in one form or another.
3. The World: This is the top row. EI is concerned with the intra and inter-dynamics of people. Leadership is also concerned with the World that the team effects.

Valuable as it is, we say there is much more to leadership than EI, though it is a very good place to start. For example: Connecting with a Vision of the World as it could be is outside the scope of Emotional Intelligence on several counts. However, the quality of the leader's Awareness and Connection, and, therefore, the quality of the Transformation the leader can effect, is greatly influenced by the quality of their Emotional Intelligence.

3D Leadership and the Integral Model

3-Dimensional Leadership is both informed by the Integral Model[60] and may even contribute to its development. At a basic level, the "I" and "We" that represent the upper and lower left hand quadrants are represented in the 3-Dimensional Model by "Self" and "Team", while the "It", while our "World" could be taken for the lower right, or indeed the upper and lower right.

To complicate things a little, the Self may view the Self experientially (Upper Left) or as the leader behaves in the World (Upper right).

While the AQAL ("All-Quadrants-All-Levels) is concerned with the health of the whole chain of consciousness at all levels, and with its development, the 3-D model hardwires "the Future" and the "Path" alongside the Present, because leaders are continually creating the future, or they aren't leading.

We look forward to considering whether and how such a perspective may sit within the AQAL model.

---

[60] Developed by Ken Wilber, see "The Theory of Everything" and other works.

Towards a Common Framework for Leadership

Leadership isn't widely understood. There remain widely divergent views as to what leadership is, let alone how it may be developed. That's what we want to remedy.

The lack of a common framework makes it hard to share and compare leadership, making leadership development harder than it need be. In the absence of a proper framework some have said this is how we do leadership around here: "lead if you will, but lead my way", a one-size fits all imposition. Others have said, find your own way.

The popularity of "situational leadership" suggests an appetite for something more but while a situational-specific approach seemed hard to refute, it didn't seem to take us much further, while the idea of "leadership styles" seemed to clash with authenticity[61].

We are aware that the leadership journey involves self-transformation, but a laissez-faire approach seemed inadequate. We wanted a framework that enabled people to be themselves.

We are aware that many approaches to leadership are empirical. We, by contrast, have worked from first principles.

We hope that the 3-Dimensional Leadership Model moves us all closer to such a common framework.

---

[61] In our view, habits, especially limiting habits stem from attitudes based on beliefs and values. Telling someone who does not believe in themselves to act like they do will make little difference.

The New Leaders and 3D Leadership

Students of leadership may be interested in how 3D Leadership relates to leadership styles described elsewhere. In The New Leaders[62], Goleman, Boyatzis and McKee present six leadership styles from the most to the least positive:

"Style"	
Visionary	A direct match. We place Visionary Leadership in the top right of the leadership map.
Coaching	Another match. We place Coaching Leadership in the middle.
Affiliative	We see Affiliative as a limited form of Adult Leadership. There is a kind of equality – we are in this together – and a kind of inequality: it's us against someone or something else.
Democratic	Democratic may be seen as a partial inversion of Coaching Leadership, since it involves all parties looking to one another.
Pace-setting	Pace-setting is an inversion of Authentic Leadership, which the authors of the New Leaders recognize can be toxic in large doses.
Commanding	This is an inversion of Adult Leadership, middle left, which is also seen as potentially toxic.

---

[62] The New Leaders, Daniel Goleman, Richard Boyatzis and Annie McKee, Little Brown, 2002. In the US published at Primal Leadership.

Appendix

Warren Bennis and 3D Leadership

Warren Bennis[63] is a leading thinker on leadership. How do his insights relate to 3-Dimensional Leadership?

Grounded Leadership	Challenging Leadership	Visionary Leadership
"Leaders keep their eyes on the horizon, not just on the bottom line"	*"Leadership is the capacity to translate vision into reality. The manager accepts the status quo; the leader challenges it."*	*"Leaders must encourage their organizations to dance to forms of music yet to be heard."*
Adult Leadership	**Coaching Leadership**	**Inspiring Leadership**
"Trust is the lubrication that makes it possible for organizations to work."	*"Good leaders make people feel that they're at the very heart of things, not at the periphery."*	*"People who cannot invent & reinvent themselves must be content with borrowed postures, second-hand ideas, fitting in instead of standing out."*
Authentic Leadership	**Journeying Leadership**	**Inspired Leadership**
"Leaders are people who do the right thing; managers are people who do things right."	*"Taking charge of your own learning is a part of taking charge of your life, which is the sine qua non in becoming an integrated person."*	*"Becoming a leader is synonymous with becoming yourself. It is precisely that simple, and it is also that difficult."*

---

[63] "On Becoming a Leader" Warren Bennis and over 20 other books.

Leadership and Values

This is not an exhaustive list. There is no official body that determines what is and what is not an acceptable value, so you can add values of your own even if they are not on the list. For the purposes of the exercise in Inspired Leadership, simply pick your top five values from the following list:

Accomplishment	Integrity
Adaptability	Learning
Clarity	Love
Coaching/mentoring	Making a difference
Commitment	Passion
Communication	Quality
Connection	Trust
Continuous improvement	Truth
Efficiency	Winning
Excellence	Wisdom
Financial stability	Survival
Fun	Respect
Happiness	Vision
Honesty	Vulnerability
Humility	Win / win / win

Appendix

A Word on Leadership Development

Leadership Development is about becoming a leader. So-called leadership skills are of limited value without the inner work.

So we don't do leadership training, for us a contradiction in terms. Just as all individuals are unique, so the leadership each individual develops is unique. How they blend the available tools with their own psychology, personality and experience will provide the cornerstone of Authentic Leadership.

At their best, leadership development activities create a space in which people can explore their own leadership, within an overall framework like the 3D Leadership Model.